THE CONSCIOUS CITIZEN

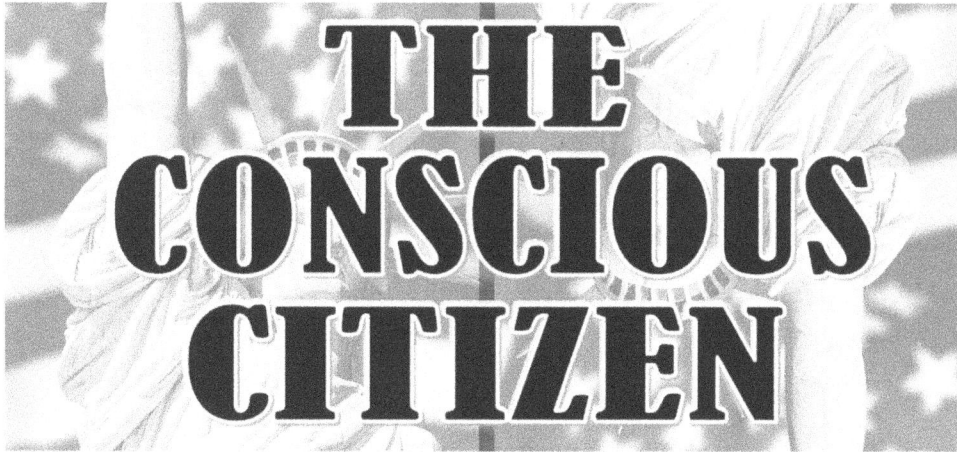

A Journey In Citizenship and The Tough Questions

A Discussion Guide

Ervin (Earl) Cobb

Published by RICHER Press
An Imprint of Richer Life, LLC
5710 Ogeechee Road, Suite 200-175, Savannah, Georgia 31405
www.richerlifellc.com

Cover Design: RICHER Media USA
Photograph: BIGSTOCK™

Volume book discounts are available for groups, companies and organizations. Contact the publisher for information and order instructions.

The Conscious Citizen
A Journey In Citizenship and The Tough Questions
A Discussion Guide

Ervin (Earl) Cobb

1. Politics & Social Sciences 2. Psychology & Counseling 3. Self-Help

(pbk : alk. Paper)

ISBN: 979-8-9863598-6-1 Paperback
ISBN: 979-8-9863598-8-5 Hardback
ISBN: 979-8-9863598-7-8 Kindle eBook
ISBN: 979-8-9863598-9-2 Discussion Guide

PRINTED IN THE UNITED STATES OF AMERICA

How To Use This Book

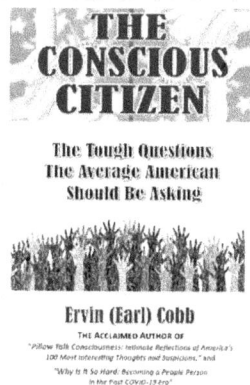

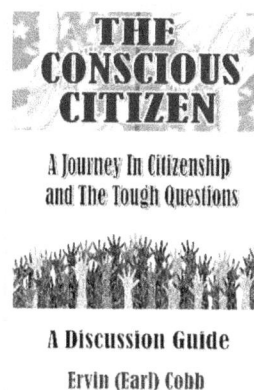

A Journey In Citizenship and The Tough Questions is a uniquely designed Discussion Guide and companion to the Master Publication, *The Conscious Citizen: The Tough Questions The Average American Should Be Asking.*

As a Discussion Guide, this publication is intended to be used by those who are reading or have read the Master Publication, with the goal of benefiting further from the insights and lessons gained on how to contribute more effectively as involved and *Conscious Citizens* within America's Democratic Republic.

The benefits are best gained by first reading the Master Publication.

Then, you should *read* and *make notes* in the Discussion Guide of any changes in your previous perspective on "how big a problem" is each of the sixteen topic areas presented following your experience of the reading of *The Conscious Citizen.*

Another approach would be to perform this exercise as a part of a neighborhood gathering or a small, facilitated group during a sponsored training session.

In either approach, you should remember that the objective is a review of the *Tough Questions* and a *discussion* of the critical thinking process used by the protagonists, Paul and Paulette, in *The Conscious Citizen,* as they arrived at their survey responses.

The objective *is not* to seek any form of *consensus*, if you are in a group setting. *It's all about understanding the thought process.* The sixteen topic areas presented in the Discussion Guide were first determined by the Pew Research Center, a well-respected and national Think Tank, as America's major "problems" in July 2024, a few months before the U.S. Presidential Election.

By spending some quality time to consciously understand, ponder, and possibly respond to each of the 114 *Tough Questions* set forward in *The Conscious Citizen,* I sincerely believe that the only result will be a *better* you, a *better* social & economic environment in the country, and a *better* future for generations to come.

Earl

THE CONSCIOUS CITIZEN

A JOURNEY IN CITIZENSHIP AND THE TOUGH QUESTIONS

Citizenship is the chance to make a difference to the place where you belong." - Charles Handy

A Journey In Citizenship and The Tough Questions

Chapter 1

HOW BIG A PROBLEM IS INFLATION IN THE COUNTRY TODAY?

"The first panacea for a mismanaged nation is inflation of the currency; the second is war. Both bring a temporary prosperity; both bring a permanent ruin. But both are the refuge of political and economic opportunists." — Ernest Hemingway

Believe it or not, here are three key and factual points about price inflation in the United States in 2024.

- The consumer price index moderated again in June 2024, according to the Bureau of Labor Statistics.
- The Consumer Price Index (CPI) annual inflation rate has declined to 3% from a 9.1% pandemic-era peak in 2022.
- Neither President Joe Biden nor former President Donald Trump shoulder much of the blame for high inflation, economists said.

Also, believe it not, Americans continue to view price inflation through their own personal lens, and the facts really don't matter.

THE TOUGH QUESTIONS
HOW BIG A PROBLEM IS INFLATION
IN THE COUNTRY TODAY?

1. Do I really understand Price Inflation within a 21st century economy the size of the United States?

   _____

   _____

   _____

   _____

   _____

   _____

2. What's causing are current Inflation rate in the U.S.?

   _____

   _____

   _____

   _____

   _____

   _____

3. Over the past few years has the rate of Inflation been on the rise or falling?

   _____

   _____

   _____

   _____

   _____

   _____

4. Who is responsible for policies designed to control inflation in the U.S.?

_____

_____

_____

_____

_____

_____

5. Should I simply blame one branch of the U.S. Government?

_____

_____

_____

_____

_____

_____

6. Since Inflation or Deflation will always exist in any free market economy, which political party has done the best job managing it in a way that impacts Americans in my income level the least?

_____

_____

_____

_____

_____

_____

7. How does the impact of the current consumer prices compare to other problems within the country at this time?

_____

_____

_____

_____

_____

_____

8. What other U.S. economic factors that I am actually "benefiting from" (i.e. higher paychecks, higher interest on savings, increase in home equity) that is helping offset some of the impacts of the ever-fluctuating rate of inflation?

_____

_____

_____

_____

_____

_____

9. How does the current U.S. Inflation rate of only 3% compare with other industrialized countries?

_____

_____

_____

_____

_____

_____

10. Since it does seem that *"the squeaky wheel gets the oil,"* is it in the best interest of the entire country for me to rank some of the other problems on the Pollster's list as bigger problems than today's Inflation rate?

_____

_____

_____

_____

_____

_____

Chapter 2

HOW BIG A PROBLEM IS THE AFFORDABILITY OF HEALTH CARE IN THE COUNTRY TODAY?

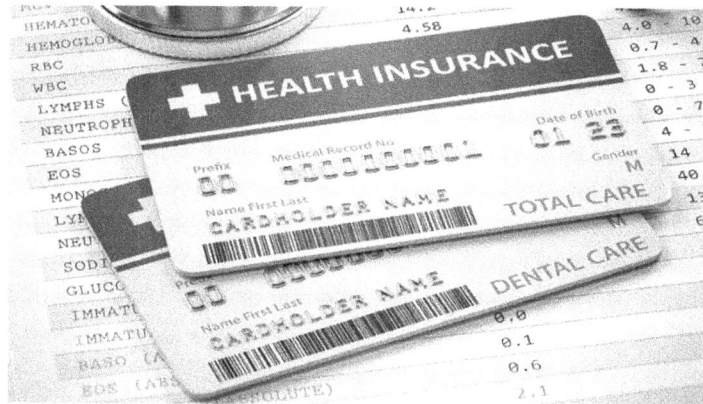

"Of all the forms of inequality, injustice in health care is the most shocking and inhuman."
— *Dr. Martin Luther King, Jr.*

Here are the Main takeaways from a KFF Tracking Poll taken in March 2022. Hopefully the insight is not shocking, and only substantiates what you, and most American, believe about the state of Healthcare in the country.

- About half of U.S. adults say it is difficult to afford health care costs, and one in four say they or a family member in their household had problems paying for health care in the past 12 months.
- The cost of health care can lead some to put off needed care.
- The cost of prescription drugs prevents some people from filling prescriptions.
- Those who are covered by health insurance are not immune to the burden of health care costs.
- Health care debt is a burden for a large share of Americans.
- Notable shares of adults still say they are worried about affording medical costs such as unexpected bills, the cost of health care services (including out-of-pocket costs not covered by insurance, such as co-pays and deductibles.

THE TOUGH QUESTIONS
HOW BIG A PROBLEM IS THE AFFORDABILITY
OF HEALTH CARE IN THE COUNTRY TODAY?

1. What is this U.S. health care *"Affordability Conundrum,"* really all about?

    _____

    _____

    _____

    _____

    _____

    _____

2. What's the actual *"bang for the buck"* of the annual U.S. health care expenditure?

    _____

    _____

    _____

    _____

    _____

    _____

3. With health care being one of the most consequential parts of the United States economy, totaling over 17%, and being such a fundamental part of supporting the health and well-being of Americans, what should I be doing, as a citizen, to help address this problem?

    _____

    _____

    _____

    _____

    _____

    _____

- Should I become a strong advocate of reducing unnecessary medical procedures? An estimated saving of $3 billion annually.
- Should I become a strong advocate of Optimizing medication use? An estimated saving of $20 billion annually.

_____

_____

_____

_____

_____

_____

4. How can I contribute to finding the societal and political courage to get around the "lobbying interest" and address the healthcare problem in a more cost-effective manner?

_____

_____

_____

_____

_____

_____

5. Is the real issue with the affordability of health care cost in the country more about the increasing delivery cost or America's culture? And can one be truly addressed without addressing the other?

_____

_____

_____

_____

_____

_____

notes

Chapter 3

HOW BIG A PROBLEM IS THE ABILITY FOR DEMOCRATS AND REPUBLICANS TO WORK TOGETHER IN THE COUNTRY TODAY?

"All people are born alike - except Republicans and Democrats. — Groucho Marx

As you may know, the creation and involvement of political parties within the United States elections and governance actually started during the Constitutional Convention.

Although, the U.S. Constitution does not mention political parties, they play an important role in U.S. government. An August 2021 Bipartisan Policy Center and Morning Consult poll found that two in three voters (67%) prefer that their member of Congress works collaboratively to achieve solutions and pass legislation. Is it an issue of "ability", "desire", or something else.

THE TOUGH QUESTIONS
HOW BIG A PROBLEM IS THE ABILITY FOR DEMOCRATS AND REPUBLICANS TO WORK TOGETHER IN THE COUNTRY TODAY?

1. Would I still vote for my Representatives if they attempted to compromise on issues that I feel strongly about. Why or Why not?

_____

_____

_____

_____

_____

_____

2. Do I understand the basis of my answer to question number one, and when was the last time I re-evaluated the reasoning and thinking in this regard?

_____

_____

_____

_____

_____

_____

3. If I would like for Republicans and Democrats to work together, what can I do to help them move in that direction?

_____

_____

_____

_____

_____

_____

4. How do I feel when I hear my Representatives spreading falsehoods, disingenuous talking points, and generating partisan hate? Is it necessary? Why?

_____

_____

_____

_____

_____

_____

5. Do I see myself as an "enabler" to the high level of political division in the country today by participating as a "good soldier" condoning Party talking points versus seeking the truth and seeking compromise?

_____

_____

_____

_____

_____

_____

6. Knowing that recent polls indicate that when most Americans say that _"they would like to see more national unity"_, they really mean that they would like for the other side to agree with them", Is this how I feel? Am I capable of keeping my thoughts and beliefs close to home, and allowing others to do the same?

_____

_____

_____

_____

_____

_____

notes

_____
_____
_____
_____
_____
_____
_____
_____
_____
_____
_____
_____
_____
_____
_____
_____
_____
_____
_____
_____
_____
_____

Chapter 4

HOW BIG A PROBLEM IS DRUG ADDICTION IN THE COUNTRY TODAY?

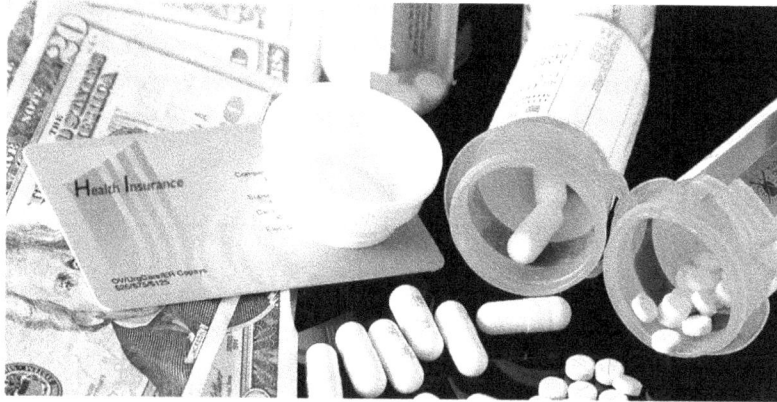

"What is addiction, really? It is a sign, a signal, a symptom of distress. It is a language that tells us about a plight that must be understood."
– Alice Miller on the true meaning of drug addiction recovery.

Either we hear about it, read about it, see the effects of it, or we are recovering from it. The it, in this case, is a *drug addiction*, also called *substance use disorder*.

You can name your substance; alcohol, nicotine, cocaine, heroin, marijuana, hashish, tobacco, barbiturates, benzodiazepines, hypnotics or opioid painkillers. The one thing they all have in common is the fact that they can be *"addictive,"* even when they are used properly. When that occurs, you are labeled as a drug addict.

When you are an addict, life becomes a problem for you, and for everyone around you. Unfortunately, this includes your friends, family members and neighbors.

According to Shatterproof, a nonprofit organization based in the United States, around 49 million Americans struggle with some type of addiction.

In an August 2023 report, the United States Department of Health and Human Services estimates that the annual economic impact of substance *"misuse"* to be $249 billion for alcohol and $193 billion for illicit drugs.

Based on all of the above, asking if drug addiction is a problem in America seems to be a "no brainer".

However, the survey question facing Paul and Paulette is *"How big a problem is drug addiction in the country today?"*

.

THE TOUGH QUESTIONS
How big a problem is Drug Addiction in the Country today?

1. If I have not experienced a drug addiction episode myself, within my family, or among any of my acquaintances, how much do I really know about the drug addiction issue in the United States, other than what I hear in the news media, or being told by others that it is a problem?

   _____

   _____

   _____

   _____

   _____

   _____

2. In my citizen advocacy activities, should I put more focus on the availability of drugs, or the need for more treatment availability across the country for those seeking help to recover from an addiction?

   _____

   _____

   _____

   _____

   _____

   _____

3. What can I do within my home and family to educate everyone on the facts and danger of drug misuse or abuse?

   _____

   _____

   _____

   _____

   _____

   _____

4. Do I know and can recognize the physical signs of abuse or addiction?

_____

_____

_____

_____

_____

_____

5. If I am aware that I have a propensity for addiction to substances or behaviors, do I know where I can seek help?

_____

_____

_____

_____

_____

_____

6. Should I be more vigilant in questioning my primary care and other physicians regarding the need for the continued use of prescription drugs; Drugs that I may no longer need based on favorable changes in health conditions or available non-pharmacological or alternative treatments?

_____

_____

_____

_____

_____

_____

7. Based on the fact that the United States spends over $600 billion annually on drug addiction and substance abuse, should I consider reducing my involvement in so-called woke social issues, [such as book banning, rolling back protections for gay and transgender students, and etc.], and increase my advocacy for the proper allocation of public funding in this area?

_____

_____

_____

_____

_____

_____

Chapter 5

HOW BIG A PROBLEM IS GUN VIOLENCE IN THE COUNTRY TODAY?

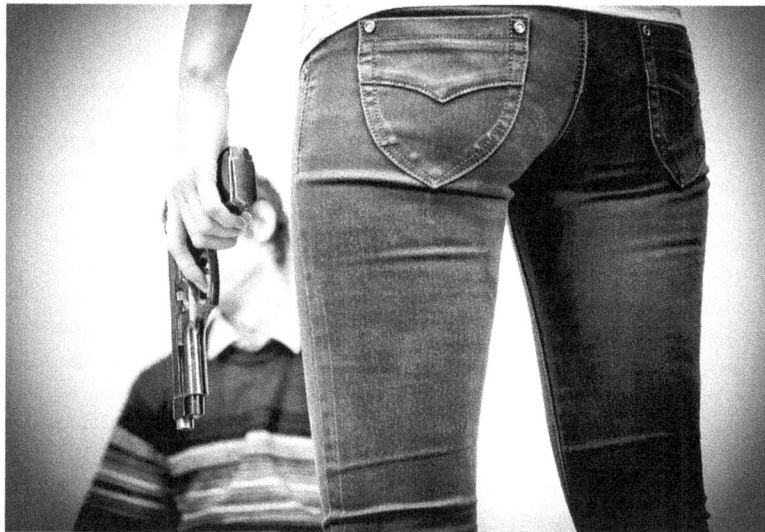

"Guns don't kill people. They make it easier." —Anonymous

Three things cannot be long hidden: the sun, the moon, and the truth. —Buddha

According to Amnesty International:

"Gun violence is violence committed with firearms, such as handguns, shotguns, or semi-automatic rifles. More than 600 people are estimated to die every day from gun violence with two-thirds of gun-related deaths, including suicides, occurring in just six countries (in descending order): Brazil, the USA, Venezuela, Mexico, India and Colombia.

Up to 71% of all homicides globally involve gun violence.

THE TOUGH QUESTIONS
HOW BIG A PROBLEM IS GUN VIOLENCE
IN THE COUNTRY TODAY?

1. As a gun owner, what are the roots of my obsession with gun ownership? And when was the last time I consciously re-evaluated them.

_____

_____

_____

_____

_____

_____

2. Is it possible for me to re-evaluate my perspective on ownership and advocacy, even if it may reduce deaths and some of the hundreds of billions of dollars currently being spent annually by the federal and state governments?

_____

_____

_____

_____

_____

_____

3. How often have I, or gun owners I know have used a firearm in self-defense?

_____

_____

_____

_____

_____

4. Am I aware of the fact that firearms are the leading cause of death for children and teens in the United States, killing more than 3,500 children annually? And, how much should I care about this fact, versus any political identity or Party affiliation I may have.

_____

_____

_____

_____

_____

_____

5. What is my primary objective to any significant and common sense gun control that would reduce the number of senseless deaths in the country, especially those from mass and school shootings?

_____

_____

_____

_____

_____

_____

6. Do I really believe the Gun Lobby's decades old, and well-advertised, gun slogan, that "any gun control" is a "slippery slope?" And do I really believe that any gun control is a first step in removing all 330 million firearms owned by over 80 million Americans?

_____

_____

_____

_____

_____

_____

notes

_____
_____
_____
_____
_____
_____
_____
_____
_____
_____
_____
_____
_____
_____
_____
_____
_____
_____
_____
_____
_____
_____
_____

Chapter 6

HOW BIG A PROBLEM IS VIOLENT CRIME IN THE COUNTRY TODAY?

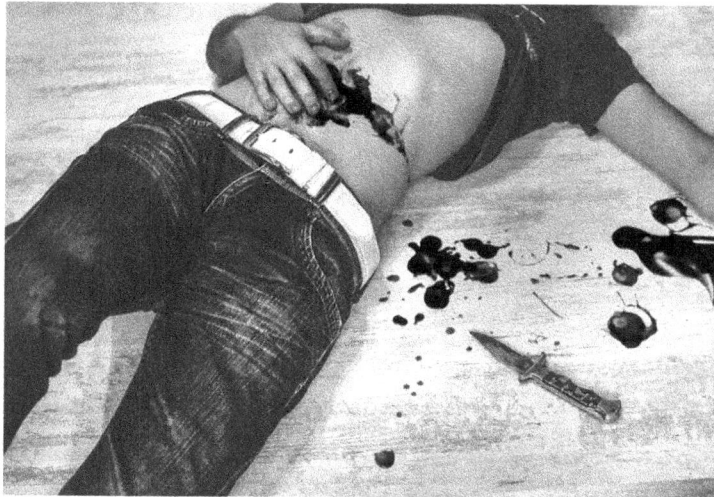

"Violence is the last refuge of the incompetent." — Isaac Asimov

According to the U.S. National Institute of Health:

"Crime victimization can impact an individual's ability to perform across a variety of roles, including those related to parenting, intimate relationships, and occupational and social functioning."

Violent crime has even more life disturbing circumstances. The circumstances can include depression; post-traumatic stress disorder; borderline personality disorder; anxiety; substance use disorders; sleep and eating disorders; and suicide.

Psychological research shows that there are four main reasons people are believed to commit violent crimes. *"1.) There is a failure in psychological development somewhere in their life, 2.) they were exposed to negative learned behaviors, 3.) they inherited negative traits, or 4.)it is related to mental illness."*

THE TOUGH QUESTIONS
HOW BIG A PROBLEM IS VIOLENT CRIME
IN THE COUNTRY TODAY?

1. Have I taken the time to understand policies and actions influencing the actual trend, falling or increasing, of the violent crime rate in the United States?

    _____

    _____

    _____

    _____

    _____

    _____

2. Contrary to fearmongering from politicians and press, indicating that American cities are experiencing record crime rates, do I know the trend of the crime rate in my city? And what's being done to address crime, in general?

    _____

    _____

    _____

    _____

    _____

    _____

3. Since much of the crime being experienced in most cities is property damage, larceny & theft, do I know what I can do to help reduce the crime rate?

    _____

    _____

    _____

    _____

    _____

    _____

4. With mental illness, homelessness and poverty being strongly associated with certain types of crimes, such as sexual assault, beatings, and robberies, should I become more of an advocate in supporting efforts to address these societal issues?

_____

_____

_____

_____

_____

_____

5. Since the facts indicates that, in general, crime in the U.S. has not been rising for years, should I be asking, *"Why aren't we, as a country, not taking common-sense measures, including gun regulations, and support for those who need medical care and stable housing, to prevent future increases in the crime rate?"*

_____

_____

_____

_____

_____

_____

notes

_____
_____
_____
_____
_____
_____
_____
_____
_____
_____
_____
_____
_____
_____
_____
_____
_____
_____
_____
_____
_____
_____

Chapter 7

HOW BIG A PROBLEM IS THE FEDERAL BUDGET DEFICIT IN THE COUNTRY TODAY?

"Our national debt after all is an internal debt owed not only by the Nation but to the Nation. If our children have to pay interest on it they will pay that interest to themselves. A reasonable internal debt will not impoverish our children or put the Nation into bankruptcy". — Franklin D. Roosevelt

"I could end the deficit in 5 minutes. You just pass a law that says that anytime there is a deficit of more than 3% of GDP all sitting members of congress are ineligible for reelection." — Warren Buffett

In my research into federal budget deficits, I learned that the United States government did not always run a deficit. Believe it or not, in the 19th century the U.S. federal government only ran deficits during wartime or during financial crises.

In the 20th century the U.S. ran a deficit during World War I, the Great Depression, World War II, and in almost all years since 1960, during peace and war.

Today, the United States is carrying a budget deficit of over $1trillion. But, in the full scheme of things — does it matter?

31

THE TOUGH QUESTIONS
How Big a Problem is the Federal Budget Deficit in the Country Today?

1. Have I taken the time to understand the U.S. Federal government's budgeting process, and am I aware of what has been driving deficit spending over the past few years?

   _____

   _____

   _____

   _____

   _____

   _____

2. Do I know the policy options that are being proposed by bipartisan groups who have already studied the federal budget deficit issue, and have proposed solutions?

   _____

   _____

   _____

   _____

   _____

   _____

3. Should I be asking my Representatives about the policy options they propose to remedy the problem of our expanding deficits and debt? Do I feel that the policy options they are proposing are new, bipartisan solutions to complex challenges or are they partisan "talking points," which continues to _blame the other party._

   _____

   _____

   _____

   _____

   _____

   _____

4. Am I familiar with the potential consequences of high federal budget deficits?

_____

_____

_____

_____

_____

_____

5. What has been the impact of the recent series of tax cuts on contributing to the Federal budget and the need for deficit spending?

_____

_____

_____

_____

_____

_____

6. Is a blanket promise by some politicians to "never raise taxes" a prudent and rational approach to ensure that our country is capable of addressing the unprecedented environmental and political challenge we face today?

_____

_____

_____

_____

_____

7. What adjustments am I willing to make in my quality of life to contribute to sufficient federal funding required to address public health, national defense and social security?

_____

_____

_____

_____

_____

notes

_____
_____
_____
_____
_____
_____
_____
_____
_____
_____
_____
_____
_____
_____
_____
_____
_____
_____
_____
_____
_____
_____

Chapter 8

HOW BIG A PROBLEM IS THE STATE OF MORAL VALUES IN THE COUNTRY TODAY?

"The United States faces many well-documented problems, from climate change and terrorism to racial injustice and economic inequality — and yet, most Americans believe their government should devote scarce resources to reversing an imaginary trend."
— Mastroianni and Gilbert, authors of The illusion of moral decline. *Nature Magazine,* 2023

I am approaching three-quarters of a century of being born in, brought up in, educated in, and living in, America; And I have come to believe that "morality" still means different things to different people.

Like many Americans, when asked about the state of morality, what comes to my mind are things like everyday kindness, honesty, and basic human decency.

However, I also believe that in the 21ˢᵗ century, with so much political focus on social divisiveness, and the ease of globally spreading any narrative one wishes via social media, a growing number of citizens respond to a question about morality with subconscious thoughts. Their views are normally not just focused on kindness, honesty, and basic human decency.

A large number of Americans base their views of morality on personal and social values, such as: divorce, extramarital affairs, gambling, abortion, alcohol use, premarital sex, and their LGBTQ neighbors.

THE TOUGH QUESTIONS
How Big a Problem is the State of Moral Values in the Country Today?

1. When I am asked about moral values, what are the first things that come to mind?

   _____

   _____

   _____

   _____

   _____

   _____

2. When was the last time I felt a need to re-evaluate my list of moral values, in light of generational and multi-cultural changes within the growing American population?

   _____

   _____

   _____

   _____

   _____

   _____

3. Since none of us chooses birth parents or the situations and circumstances into which we are born and raised, why should I expect others to have the same set of life principles and standards as me, and those with whom I now surround myself with?

   _____

   _____

   _____

   _____

   _____

   _____

4. If the principles and standards of my neighbors do not infringe upon me and my family, why do I feel the need to rally behind social causes, which berates and marginalizes them?

_____

_____

_____

_____

_____

_____

5. Since all social norms are shared expectations of behavior for specific situations and hinges on the belief of *"right and wrong,"* if someone else's behaviors are not "illegal," what convinces me that *I am so right* or *they are so wrong,* to the degree, that I am motivated, to change the laws to fit my beliefs and ignore theirs?

_____

_____

_____

_____

_____

_____

notes

Chapter 9

HOW BIG A PROBLEM IS THE QUALITY OF PUBLIC K-12 SCHOOLS IN THE COUNTRY TODAY?

"The whole idea of public education was to train young people about how our system of government works, so they could be good citizens and be part of it. We're not doing that today." — Sandra Day O'Connor

According to Fortune, American students are facing four main challenges in public schools today, they are:

1. **Reading:** A third of young students are behind in reading.
2. **Math:** Only 36% of fourth graders are proficient in grade-level math.
3. **History:** Eighth graders' history scores on the National Assessment for Educational Progress (NAEP) are the lowest since 1994; and
4. **Teacher shortages**: Every state experienced teacher shortages in at least one subject in 2022.

Also, in terms of the quality of K-12 education in our country, recently released data from international math and science assessments indicate that students in the United States continue to rank around the middle of the pack, and behind many other advanced industrial nations.

According to The Center for Education Policy:

"The Founding Fathers maintained that the success of the fragile American democracy would depend on the competency of its citizens. They believed strongly that preserving democracy would require an educated population that could understand political and social issues and would participate in civic life, vote wisely, protect their rights and freedoms, and resist tyrants and demagogues. Character and virtue were also considered essential to good citizenship, and education was seen as a means to provide moral instruction and build character."

THE TOUGH QUESTIONS
HOW BIG A PROBLEM IS THE QUALITY OF PUBLIC K-12 SCHOOLS IN THE COUNTRY TODAY?

1. Since I have school age children, do I know the academic approach and curriculum of the K-12 schools in my community?

_____

_____

_____

_____

_____

_____

2. Do I believe that parents should have more or less involvement in the K-12 school curriculum? Why? or Why not?

_____

_____

_____

_____

_____

_____

3. Do I believe that parents know more than trained educators and educational specialist about the curriculum and books required to provide K-12 students with a quality and globally competitive education? If yes, why?

_____

_____

_____

_____

_____

4. I don't have school age children, why is it important to know the academic approach, curriculum, delinquency, and dropout rates of the K-12 schools in my community?

_____

_____

_____

_____

_____

_____

_____

5. As a senior citizen, why should I be concerned about the quality of K-12 schools in my community? And wouldn't more school funding just force me to pay more in taxes?

_____

_____

_____

_____

_____

_____

6. According the Georgetown University's McCourt School of Public Policy, as of March 2023, 32 states provide an estimated $6.2 billion in subsidies to private schools through various programs, including tuition vouchers, education savings accounts, and tax-credit scholarships. Do I know how this is impacting the quality of public K-12 schools in the U.S. and in my community?

_____

_____

_____

_____

_____

_____

notes

_____

_____

_____

_____

_____

_____

_____

_____

_____

_____

_____

_____

_____

_____

_____

_____

_____

_____

_____

_____

_____

Chapter 10

HOW BIG A PROBLEM IS ILLEGAL IMMIGRATION IN THE COUNTRY TODAY?

"My fellow Americans, we are and always will be a nation of immigrants. We were strangers once, too." — Barack Obama

We all hear the two words mentioned a lot, but exactly, what is an *illegal immigrant?*

We also often hear phrases like, *"Control the border," "Protect the border," "Close the border", "Build the wall," "Fix the immigration problem,"* and *"We need immigration reform."* They all have become daily talking points for talk radio, cable television and for politicians, during every presidential year for decades.

We also frequently are reminded that, *"We are a nation of immigrants."* Some of you may be surprised to know that:

- The phrase *"We are a nation of immigrants"* was actually *not* coined until the decades of the Civil War; and
- The United States Constitution doesn't explicitly mention immigration, but it does address related topics that give Congress the power to regulate immigration.

The United States Department of Homeland Security, or DHS, is the Government agency responsible for improving the security of the United States. The department's responsibilities include Customs, Border, and Immigration enforcement.

43

According to DHS:

"The unauthorized resident immigrant population is defined as all foreign-born non-citizens who are not legal residents. Most unauthorized residents either entered the United States without inspection or were admitted temporarily and stayed past the date they were required to leave."

Some of the problems with illegal or unauthorized immigrants are defined by American immigration groups, like the Federation for American Immigration Reform.

In their words, *Illegal Immigration:*

- Threatens our national sovereignty.
- Undermines the rule of law.
- Undercuts legal immigration.
- Contributes to unsustainable population growth, affecting the environment.
- Harms American workers.
- Threatens Americans' safety and well-being; and
- Is a burden on the taxpayer.

While other American immigration activists, like the Center for Budget and Policy Priorities, share different beliefs about the American immigrant population, in general. This group espouses that: In fact, immigrants contribute to the U.S. economy in many ways.

- Immigrants work at high rates and make up more than a third of the workforce in some industries.
- Their geographic mobility helps local economies respond to worker shortages, smoothing out bumps that could otherwise weaken the economy.
- Immigrant workers help support the aging native-born population, increasing the number of workers as compared to retirees and bolstering the Social Security and Medicare trust funds; and
- Children born to immigrant families are upwardly mobile, promising future benefits not only to their families, but to the U.S. economy overall.

So, as you can see, the topic of *Illegal Immigration* in America today can truly be characterized as a "hot potato." Of course, the phrase "hot potato" is often used in politics to describe controversial or sensitive issues that are difficult, and uncomfortable, for people to deal with.

THE TOUGH QUESTIONS
HOW BIG A PROBLEM IS ILLEGAL IMMIGRATION IN THE COUNTRY TODAY?

1. Am I aware of any illegal immigration issues in my city or region? If so, how does it affect me.

   _____

   _____

   _____

   _____

   _____

   _____

2. Should I question the costs and motives when I see my state officials sending national guard troops to border states when Immigration is a Federal government issue and responsibility?

   _____

   _____

   _____

   _____

   _____

   _____

3. Do I know how the U.S. government is handling the situation at the border? What is causing the migration surge? How could the immigration system be improved?

   _____

   _____

   _____

   _____

   _____

   _____

4. Do I know why the Department of Homeland Security detains illegal immigrants in the U.S., and what alternatives are available?

_____

_____

_____

_____

_____

_____

5. Do I know what rights illegal immigrants have once they are in the United States?

_____

_____

_____

_____

_____

_____

6. Do I know the truthful and unbiased answers to security concerns associated with the migrant influx, such as crime, terrorism, and drugs?

_____

_____

_____

_____

_____

7. How can new technologies like AI and biometric sensors improve efficiency and accuracy while also protecting migrants' privacy?

_____

_____

_____

_____

_____

_____

8. Do I believe the United States should make it easier or harder for people to immigrate legally?

_____

_____

_____

_____

_____

_____

_____

_____

_____

_____

_____

notes

Chapter 11

HOW BIG A PROBLEM IS CLIMATE CHANGE IN THE COUNTRY TODAY?

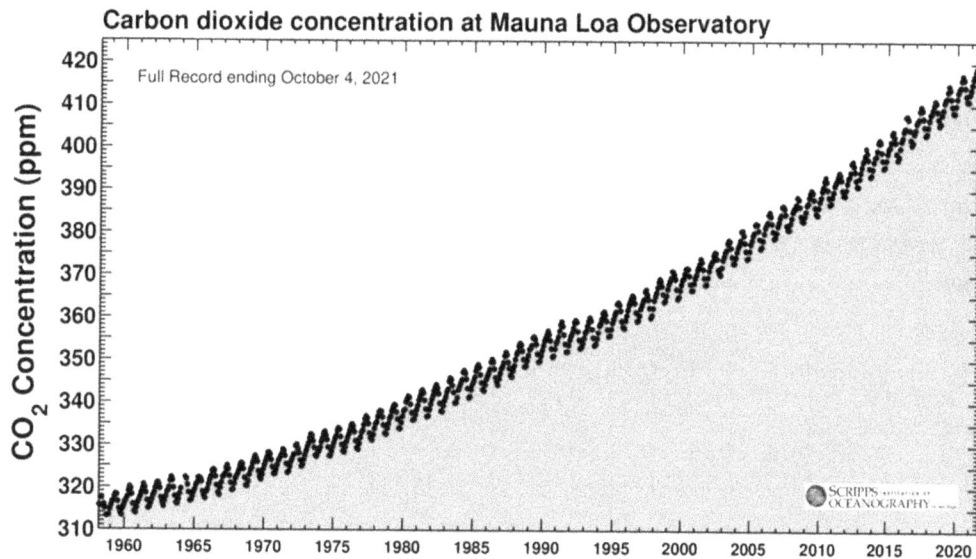

Carbon dioxide concentration at Mauna Loa Observatory

Full Record ending October 4, 2021

About the picture above. Measurements of the amount of carbon dioxide in water and in the air, made over five years in the 1950s and 60s by Charles David Keeling, provided unequivocal proof that carbon dioxide concentrations were rising. It led to the Keeling Curve, which has documented daily changes in carbon dioxide levels for over six decades. Keeling's discovery is acknowledged as one of the most important scientific works of the 20th century. Source: UK Research and Innovation

According to the United Nations, *"Climate change refers to long-term shifts in temperatures and weather patterns. Such shifts can be natural, due to changes in the sun's activity or large volcanic eruptions. But since the 1800s, human activities have been the main driver of climate change, primarily due to the burning of fossil fuels like coal, oil and gas."*

I am sure you will agree with me that to truly understand *Climate Change*, it's causes, and it's possible effects on *long-term shifts in temperatures and weather patterns* on Earth, during our lifetime, can be challenging. I have learned that the best courses of study to adequately educate yourself on *Climate Change* are college level courses in science, engineering, and climatology.

And, according to Forbes, *only about half (54.3%) of working-age adults in the U.S. have a college degree or other postsecondary credentials.*

So, when a pollster ask a question like, "How Big a Problem is Climate Change in the Country Today," we can expect varying opinions, and at least half of Americans to respond based on:

49

1. A superficial level of knowledge about the topic.
2. What they have heard in the news media and from speaking with family, friends and acquaintances; and
3. Their beliefs as a part of organizations with strong political leanings on the subject in one direction or the other. Especially since the global fossil fuel and land development industries have both a tremendous stake and role to play in this issue.

To anyone exposed to the national and international news media, and the politics surrounding *Climate Change*, this should not be a surprise.

The findings of a 2016 survey of *American's Views on Climate Change and Climate Scientists*, conducted by the Pew Research Center includes the following:

"There is a host of ways Americans' opinions about climate issues divide. The divisions start with views about the causes of global climate change. The disputes extend to differing views about the likely impact of climate change and the possible remedies, both at the policy level and the level of personal behavior."

THE TOUGH QUESTIONS
How big a problem is Climate Change in the Country today?

1. Have I spent the time to understand climate change and put the evidence that climate change is happening in proper perspective?

_____

_____

_____

_____

_____

_____

2. What do I believe is the cause of climate change and Why?

_____

_____

_____

_____

_____

_____

3. Am I fully aware of the consequences of climate change?

_____

_____

_____

_____

_____

_____

4. Do I know what I can do to help mitigate climate change?

_____

_____

_____

_____

_____

_____

5. Do I know if my elected officials' position on climate change and do I agree with that position? Why or Why not?

_____

_____

_____

_____

_____

_____

6. Do I feel that it is important to support political candidates who do not share my beliefs regarding climate change? Why or Why not?

_____

_____

_____

_____

_____

_____

7. Do I know why I should be concerned about a degree or two change in the average global temperature?

_____

_____

_____

_____

_____

_____

8. Do I know how climate change can affect my health, and the health of my family?

_____

_____

_____

_____

_____

_____

9. Do I know who is most at risk from the impacts of climate change?

_____

_____

_____

_____

_____

_____

10. Do I know the benefits of taking action to help prevent greenhouse gases from exceeding dangerous levels now?

_____

_____

_____

_____

_____

_____

Chapter 12

HOW BIG A PROBLEM IS RACISM IN THE COUNTRY TODAY?

What is racism? Let's start with an excerpt from a 2003 article titled, *"The Historical Origins and Development of Racism"* written by George M. Fredrickson, the Edgar E. Robinson Professor Emeritus of United States History at Stanford University.

"Racism exists when one ethnic group or historical collectivity dominates, excludes, or seeks to eliminate another on the basis of differences that it believes are hereditary and unalterable. An ideological basis for explicit racism came to a unique fruition in the West during the modern period. No clear and unequivocal evidence of racism has been found in other cultures or in Europe before the Middle Ages. The identification of the Jews with the devil and witchcraft in the popular mind of the thirteenth and fourteenth centuries was perhaps the first sign of a racist view of the world. Official sanction for such attitudes came in sixteenth century Spain when Jews who had converted to Christianity and their descendants became the victims of a pattern of discrimination and exclusion."

I feel that the most intellectual and candid approach to anchor a discussion where the word "racism" is the *elephant in the room,* is to first accurately introduce the elephant.

According to the American Psychological Association:

"Racism is a form of prejudice that generally includes negative emotional reactions to members of a group, acceptance of negative stereotypes, and racial discrimination against individuals."

Hopefully the history presented in the above excerpt, on the origin of racism within human societies is not news to most of you.

What may be news is the fact that genetic studies in the late twentieth century refuted the existence of biogenetically distinct races, and scholars now argue that "races" are *cultural interventions* reflecting specific attitudes and beliefs that were imposed on different populations in the wake of western European conquests beginning in the 15th century.

Therefore, I am fairly confident that when most Americans are asked the question, *"How Big a Problem is Racism in the Country Today,"* there will be varying interpretations and views on what they believe are racist actions, racist behaviors, and racist consequences.

And I am one-hundred percent confident that based on their personal life experience, their level of domestic and international exposure, their degree of honesty, and maybe their political leaning, each of them would be true to their belief.

So, in my opinion, pollsters and those relying on national polls with a general question concerning *Americans* and *Racism*, have a difficult job interpreting reliable and actionable results.

As I think more about this particular survey question, I am reminded of a quote attributed to Thomas Sowell, an American economist, social philosopher, and political commentator, when he once said.

"The word racism is like ketchup. It can be put on practically anything - and demanding evidence makes you a racist."

THE TOUGH QUESTIONS
How Big a Problem is Racism in the Country Today?

1. As a White American, how do I speak to my White friends about their racist beliefs?

_____

_____

_____

_____

_____

_____

2. How much do I personally worry about race relations?

_____

_____

_____

_____

_____

_____

3. Do I understand the concept of white privilege and why is this important to understand systemic racism in America?

_____

_____

_____

_____

_____

_____

4. I don't see color in people, and I consider myself colorblind. What's wrong with that?

_____

_____

_____

_____

_____

5. Do I know how to explain systemic racism and racial inequality to my family, friends and others?

_____

_____

_____

_____

_____

6. Do I know why talking about race and racism matters?

_____

_____

_____

_____

_____

7. I'm a White American who wants to help combat racism. Where do I start?

_____

_____

_____

_____

_____

8. I'm not a White American who wants to help combat racism. Where do I start?

_____

_____

_____

_____

_____

notes

_____
_____
_____
_____
_____
_____
_____
_____
_____
_____
_____
_____
_____
_____
_____
_____
_____
_____
_____
_____
_____
_____

notes

_____
_____
_____
_____
_____
_____
_____
_____
_____
_____
_____
_____
_____
_____
_____
_____
_____
_____
_____
_____
_____
_____

Chapter 13

HOW BIG A PROBLEM IS DOMESTIC TERRORISM IN THE COUNTRY TODAY?

"Terrorism has become the systematic weapon of a war that knows no borders or seldom has a face."
— Jacques Chirac

Domestic terrorism is not a new threat in the United States, yet it is a threat Americans have endured too often in recent years. Incidents of domestic terrorism in the United States increased by 357% between 2013 and 2021. The Federal Bureau of Investigations and the U. S. Department of Homeland Security are charged with collaborating to prevent domestic threats.

According to the U.S. Department of Homeland Security:

"There were 231 domestic terrorism incidents between 2010 and 2021. Of these, about 35% (the largest category) were classified as racially- or ethnically motivated. More recently, in May 2022, a racially motivated individual shot and killed 10 people in Buffalo, New York. Anti-government or anti-authority motivated violent extremism was the second largest category of incidents, and resulted in 15 deaths over the same time period."

I just wonder how worried are most Americans that someone in their family will become a victim of domestic terrorism.

THE TOUGH QUESTIONS
HOW BIG A PROBLEM IS DOMESTIC TERRORISM IN THE COUNTRY TODAY?

1. Do I know how domestic terrorism in the U.S. is defined?

    _____
    _____
    _____
    _____
    _____
    _____

2. How much do I know about the U.S. campaign against terrorism?

    _____
    _____
    _____
    _____
    _____
    _____

3. Why should I always be aware of the U S. Homeland Security Advisory System Threat Level for domestic terrorism?

    _____
    _____
    _____
    _____
    _____
    _____

4. Do I know where I should report suspicious activity which might lead to an act of domestic terrorism?

_____

_____

_____

_____

_____

_____

5. Are my Congressional Representatives sharing sufficient details regarding potential domestic terrorism risk during townhall meetings?

_____

_____

_____

_____

_____

_____

6. Am I under the impression that "terrorists are always (brown) Muslims and "white people are never terrorists?" Why? Or Why not?

_____

_____

_____

_____

_____

_____

notes

_____
_____
_____
_____
_____
_____
_____
_____
_____
_____
_____
_____
_____
_____
_____
_____
_____
_____
_____
_____
_____
_____

Chapter 14

HOW BIG A PROBLEM IS CONDITIONS OF ROADS, BRIDGES AND OTHER INFRASTRUCTURE IN THE COUNTRY TODAY?

"Unlike China, American roads and transport systems have been around for too many decades. We need to fix them, not dream of gleaming new ones." —Aaron M. Renn

I believe that many of you would agree with me that it would be an understatement to say that most of America's roads, bridges and public infrastructure are aging. Too many of them are beyond aging.

I am sure that most of you are aware of the infrastructure-related events that have occurred in the United States recently. From the collapse of the Baltimore, Maryland bridge to the crumbling of a section of Interstate 95, and the collapse of buildings in various cities across the country, it is quite obvious.

According to the U.S. Army Corps of Engineers and the American Society of Civil Engineers:

"The average life of a significant piece of infrastructure is 50 years. The average age of a US bridge is 44 years, 45 for significant pipes and 57 for dams. There is a significant backlog of underfunded projects in the United States. In 2023 alone, almost $45 billion was spent by the federal government, and another $82 billion was spent by individual states for infrastructure updates."

U.S. Invests Less in Transportation Than Other Developed Countries, China

Annual inland infrastructure investment as a percentage of GDP, selected countries

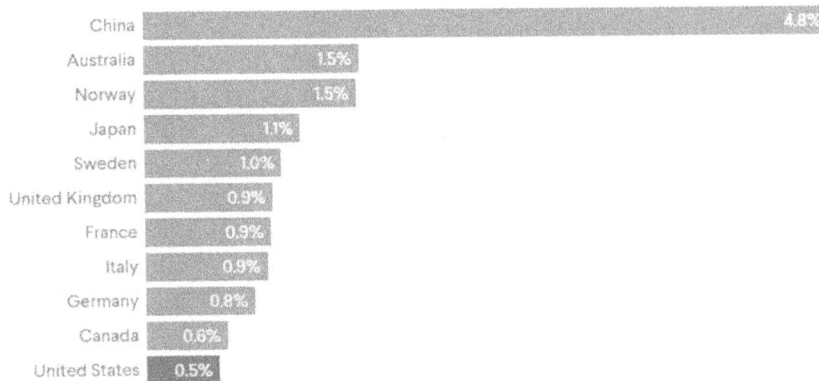

Country	Percentage
China	4.8%
Australia	1.5%
Norway	1.5%
Japan	1.1%
Sweden	1.0%
United Kingdom	0.9%
France	0.9%
Italy	0.9%
Germany	0.8%
Canada	0.6%
United States	0.5%

Note: Data is from 2021 or the most recent year available. Inland infrastructure includes roads, rail, inland waterways, maritime ports, and airports. All sources of financing are accounted for.

Source: Organization for Economic Cooperation and Development.

COUNCIL on
FOREIGN
RELATIONS

In spite of the obvious needs for repair and replacement, the chart above from the *Council on Foreign Relations* shows that in 2021, the U.S. only invested 0.5 percent of GDP in transportation infrastructure, including roads, rails and waterways. This compares to China's 4.8% and Japan's 1.1%.

I am also sure that most of you are aware that the primary contributor to America's infrastructure was President Dwight Eisenhower. Eisenhower, the Supreme Allied Commander during World War II, realized how vital a robust highway system is to a country's productivity and national defense from seeing America's original shortfalls during the war. So, the 34th President signed the Federal Aid Highway Act in 1956. This major investment created more accessible transportation and travel throughout the country. This not only provided accessibility to millions of people, but it also produced thousands and thousands of jobs. However, as the year of the passing of the Act shows, 1956 was 68 years ago.

THE TOUGH QUESTIONS
HOW BIG A PROBLEM IS CONDITIONS OF ROADS, BRIDGES AND OTHER INFRASTRUCTURE IN THE COUNTRY TODAY?

1. Do I know how important infrastructure is to the U.S. economy?

_____
_____
_____
_____
_____
_____

2. Am I aware of the history of how most of America's inland infrastructure was expanded in the 1950's and why such a major investment was made?

_____
_____
_____
_____
_____
_____

3. Do I really know the condition and maintenance needs of our nation's infrastructure?

_____
_____
_____
_____
_____
_____

4. Do I know what percent of Gross Domestic Product or GDP that the U.S. invests in transportation infrastructure, including roads, rails and waterways annually, as compared to other countries?

_____

_____

_____

_____

_____

_____

5. Do I know why the United States generally lags behind its peers in the developed world in infrastructure repair and maintenance ?

_____

_____

_____

_____

_____

_____

6. Have I asked my legislative Representatives how they voted on the 2021 infrastructure Bill? If not, why?

_____

_____

_____

_____

_____

_____

7. What should I be doing to encourage my legislators to do more and support legislation to repair and replace our nations crumbling roads, bridges and other infrastructure?

_____

_____

_____

_____

_____

_____

notes

_____
_____
_____
_____
_____
_____
_____
_____
_____
_____
_____
_____
_____
_____
_____
_____
_____
_____
_____
_____
_____
_____
_____

Chapter 15

HOW BIG A PROBLEM IS INTERNATIONAL TERRORISM IN THE COUNTRY TODAY?

"The object of terrorism is terrorism. The object of oppression is oppression. The object of torture is torture. The object of murder is murder. The object of power is power. Now do you begin to understand me?" — George Orwell

According to a report by the Chicago Council on Global Affairs, *"In 2002, nine in 10 Americans saw international terrorism as a critical threat. About six in 10 do today."* It appears that in the almost 23 years since the September 11 attacks against the World Trade Center and the Pentagon, Americans' memories of 9/11 and concerns about international terrorism have declined significantly.

The key findings of this September 2020 report on Americans' concerns regarding international terrorism included the following:

- *"Nearly six in 10 Americans (58%) classify international terrorism as a critical threat to the United States.*

- *Equal portions of Republicans (60%), Democrats (59%), and Independents (55%) classify terrorism as a critical threat.*

- *While the perceived threat posed by international terrorism has declined significantly over the last two decades, it still remains a top concern in the minds of Americans compared to other potential international threats."*

Americans watched in horror as the terrorist attacks of September 11, 2001, left nearly 3,000 people dead in New York City, Washington, D.C., and Shanksville, Pennsylvania.

71

However, what was the enduring power of the 9/11 attacks? Also, how does the memory of those attacks feed into how big a problem many Americans believe international terrorism is today?

As the chart below from the Pew Research Center shows, an overwhelming share of Americans who are old enough to recall the day, remember where they were, and what they were doing when they heard the news. Yet, an ever-growing number of Americans have no personal memory of that day, either because they were too young or not yet born.

9/11 a powerful memory for Americans – but only for adults old enough to remember

% who say they remember exactly where they were or what they were doing the moment they heard the news about the Sept. 11 attacks

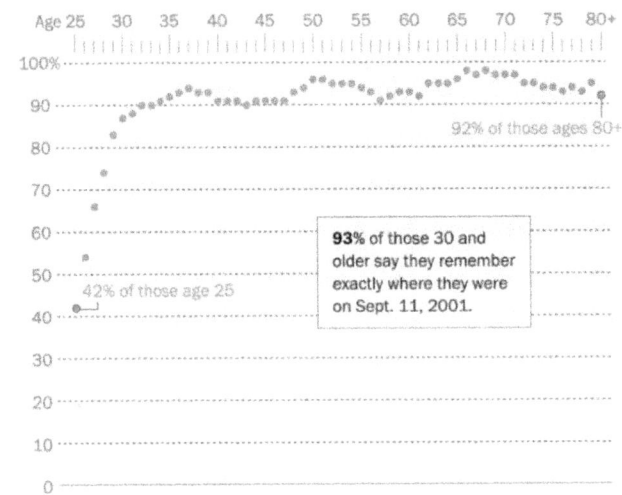

92% of those ages 80+

93% of those 30 and older say they remember exactly where they were on Sept. 11, 2001.

42% of those age 25

Note: Data shown for individual ages based on rolling five-year average by age.
Source: Survey of U.S. adults conducted Aug. 23-29, 2021

PEW RESEARCH CENTER

THE TOUGH QUESTIONS
HOW BIG A PROBLEM IS INTERNATIONAL TERRORISM IN THE COUNTRY TODAY?

1. Do I know how the United States defines terrorism?

    _____
    _____
    _____
    _____
    _____
    _____

2. Do I know who is responsible for protecting the United States and its citizens from terrorism?

    _____
    _____
    _____
    _____
    _____
    _____

3. Do I know the national strategy for anti-terrorism?

    _____
    _____
    _____
    _____
    _____
    _____

4. Do I know why it is important to be knowledgeable of international anti-terrorism laws.

_____

_____

_____

_____

_____

_____

5. Am I aware of the international framework available to help me understand if any acts I have observed are terrorist in nature or not?

_____

_____

_____

_____

_____

6. Do I really know why international law is important in Counterterrorism?

_____

_____

_____

_____

_____

7. Do I know what the possible international terrorist threats to the vital interests of the United States are?

_____

_____

_____

_____

_____

_____

8. Do I know how terrorism can affect the international market?

_____

_____

_____

_____

_____

_____

notes

_____
_____
_____
_____
_____
_____
_____
_____
_____
_____
_____
_____
_____
_____
_____
_____
_____
_____
_____
_____
_____
_____
_____

Chapter 16

HOW BIG A PROBLEM IS UNEMPLOYMENT IN THE COUNTRY TODAY?

"To rule a country of a thousand chariots, there must be reverent attention to business, and sincerity; economy in expenditure, and love for men; and the employment of the people at the proper seasons."
— Confucius

According to the U.S. Department of Labor's, Bureau of Labor Statistics, *"The unemployment rate rose to 4.3 percent in July 2024, and nonfarm payroll employment edged up by 114,000, the U.S. Bureau of Labor Statistics reported today. Employment continued to trend up in health care, in construction, and in transportation and warehousing, while information lost jobs."*

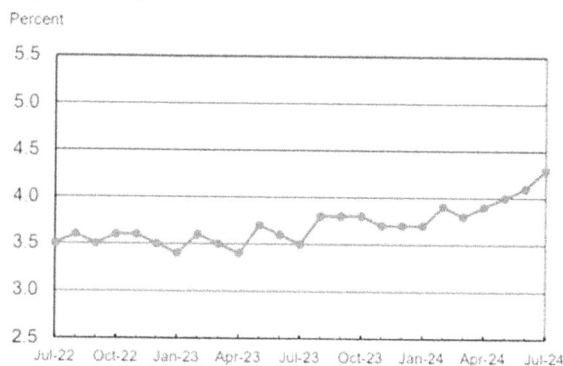

Chart 1. Unemployment rate, seasonally adjusted, July 2022 – July 2024

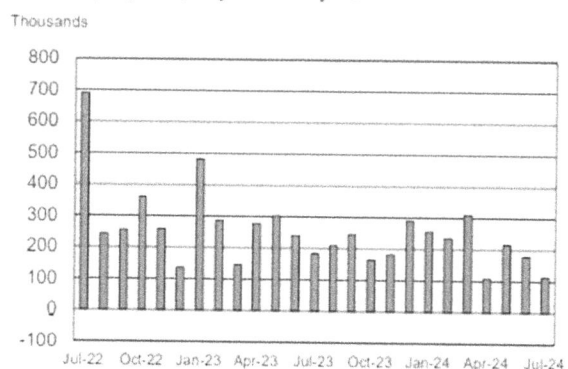

Chart 2. Nonfarm payroll employment over-the-month change, seasonally adjusted, July 2022 – July 2024

In the ever evolving and changing landscape of the job market, unemployment is an unfortunate reality that many individuals have to face at some point in their lives.

Beyond the financial strain, unemployment can significantly impact a person's mental well-being and overall life satisfaction.

Below is a chart by Statista, showing the total employment, and the unemployment rate in the United States from 1980 to 2023, with projections until 2029. As you can see, it reflects a constant growth in employment, and, as expected, short peaks in unemployment during periodic economic recessions.

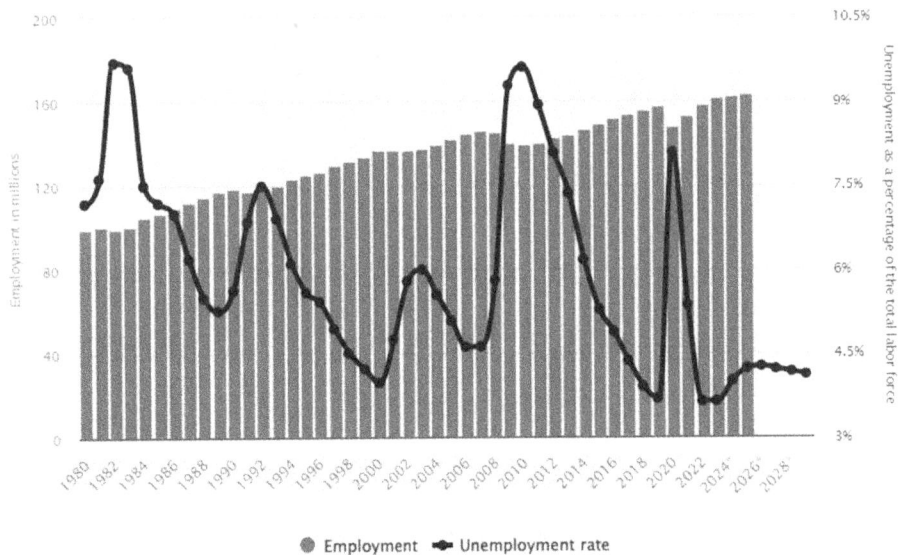

Employment ● Unemployment rate

Most headlines at the mid-point of 2024 have reflected, *Rising Wages and Historic Small Business Growth Add to Strong American Economy*.

And according to the U.S. Labor Department's Bureau of Labor Statistics, *"consumer prices dropped 0.1% in June 2024, with core inflation being the lowest in more than three years. In addition, the U.S. economy added 206,000 jobs in June 2024, exceeding expectations. In total, 15.7 million jobs have been created under President Biden."*

THE TOUGH QUESTIONS
HOW BIG A PROBLEM IS UNEMPLOYMENT IN THE COUNTRY TODAY?

1. Do I know the trend in the national and my state's unemployment numbers for the past 10 years? and have I thought about how the trend should be factored into my perception of the economy?

    _____
    _____
    _____
    _____
    _____
    _____

2. Am I aware of all the factors that contribute to unemployment rate fluctuations?

    _____
    _____
    _____
    _____
    _____
    _____

3. Do I know why there are two monthly measures of employment?

    _____
    _____
    _____
    _____
    _____
    _____

4. Do I know if undocumented immigrants are counted in the surveys?

_____

_____

_____

_____

_____

_____

5. Do I know why the establishment survey used to obtain the unemployment data have revisions?

_____

_____

_____

_____

_____

_____

6. Do I know if the establishment survey sample include small firms?

_____

_____

_____

_____

_____

_____

_____

_____

_____

_____

_____

7. Do I know how the establishment survey accounts for employment from new businesses?

_____

_____

_____

_____

_____

_____

8. Do I know if the counting process of unemployed people is limited to just those receiving unemployment insurance benefits?

_____

_____

_____

_____

_____

9. Do I know if the official unemployment rate excludes people who want a job, but are not currently looking for work?

_____

_____

_____

_____

_____

_____

_____

_____

_____

_____

_____

10. Do I know how unusually severe weather can affect employment and hours estimates?

_____

_____

_____

_____

_____

_____

RESULTS SUMMARY

DATE: _____

"Would you say each of the following is _____ in the country today."

	A Very Big Problem	A Moderately Big Problem	A Small Problem	Not a Problem at All
Inflation				
The affordability of health care				
The ability of Dems and Reps to work together				
Drug addition				
Gun violence				
Violent crime				
The federal budget deficit				
The state of moral values				
The Quality of public K-12 schools				
Illegal immigration				
Climate change				
Racism				
Domestic terrorism				
Conditions of roads, bridges and other infrastructure				
International terrorism				
Unemployment				

RESULTS SUMMARY

DATE: _____

"Would you say each of the following is _____ in the country today."

	A Very Big Problem	A Moderately Big Problem	A Small Problem	Not a Problem at All
Inflation				
The affordability of health care				
The ability of Dems and Reps to work together				
Drug addition				
Gun violence				
Violent crime				
The federal budget deficit				
The state of moral values				
The Quality of public K-12 schools				
Illegal immigration				
Climate change				
Racism				
Domestic terrorism				
Conditions of roads, bridges and other infrastructure				
International terrorism				
Unemployment				

ABOUT THE AUTHOR

ERVIN (EARL) COBB

Earl is an accomplished corporate executive, leadership development coach, lecturer, and author.

He has held senior technical and leadership positions within Fortune 100, Mid-market and Venture companies including *Honeywell, Inc.*, *Motorola, Inc.*, *The Reynolds and Reynolds Company* and *Wells Fargo Bank*. He is the former President, COO and CEO of the high-tech start-up, *MedContrax, Inc.*

Earl earned a Bachelor of Science degree in Electrical Engineering, with honors, from *Tennessee State University*. He graduated from *Arizona State University* with a Master of Science degree in Engineering.

He is a former Adjunct Professor of Management at the Keller Graduate School of Management of *DeVry University*. He has completed graduate studies at *Stanford University's Graduate School of Business*, *the Sloan School of Management at MIT* and the *Center for Creative Leadership*.

Earl is the author of 14 published books and over 100 published articles.

Other Books By
ERVIN (EARL) COBB

Living a More Thoughtful Life
Thinkable Thoughts and Relevant Reflections

Why Is It So Hard
Becoming a People Person in the Post COVID-19 Era

Situations and Leadership
Short Stories and Lifelong Lessons

Leadership Front and Center
A Decade of Thought and Tutelage

The SMART LEADER and the Skinny Principles
How to Win and Lead within Any Organization

Driving Ultimate Project Performance
Transforming from Project Manager to Project Leader

**The Official Leadership Checklist and Diary
for Project Management Professionals**

The Leadership Advantage
Do More. Lead More. Earn More.

God's Goodness & Our Mindfulness
Responding versus Reacting to Life Changing Circumstances

Focused Leadership
What You Can Do Today To Become a More Effective Leader

Pillow Talk Consciousness
Intimate Reflections on America's 100 Most Interesting
Thoughts and Suspicions

Navigating the Life Enrichment Model™

Living a Richer Life
Getting the Most out of Life's Gifts and Circumstances

The Conscious Citizen
The Tough Questions The Average American Should Be Asking